C000246244

A HERRING FAMINE

BY THE SAME AUTHOR

In the Flesh

When Love Speaks: Poetry and prose for weddings, relationships and married life (editor)

A HERRING FAMINE

Adam O'Riordan

Chatto & Windus
LONDON

1 3 5 7 9 10 8 6 4 2

Chatto & Windus, an imprint of Vintage,
20 Vauxhall Bridge Road,
London SW1V 2SA

Chatto & Windus is part of the Penguin Random House group of companies
whose addresses can be found at global.penguinrandomhouse.com

 Penguin
Random House
UK

Copyright © Adam O'Riordan 2017

Adam O'Riordan has asserted his right to be identified as the author of this Work
in accordance with the Copyright, Designs and Patents Act 1988

First published by Chatto and Windus in 2017

www.vintage-books.co.uk

A CIP catalogue record for this book is available from the British Library

ISBN 9780701187972

Typeset in India by Thomson Digital Pvt Ltd, Noida, Delhi
Printed and bound in Great Britain by Clays Ltd, St Ives plc

Penguin Random House is committed to a sustainable future for our business,
our readers and our planet. This book is made from Forest Stewardship Council®
certified paper.

For Alex, as promised

Contents

A HERRING FAMINE

Crossing the Meadow

You crossed the meadow once before,
alone that time, at night,
the ring road in the distance
gathering voice,

the sleeping ponies, thinned by winter,
still as standing stones, the clouds
of breath as you moved among
the broken circle they had formed.

I came with you in early spring
before the buttercups,
birds-foot trefoil, white clover, yarrow,
across the mudflats

a goose receding into boggy underfoot,
bloody gristle and yellowed bone,
the feather line of its splayed wing
opened to the heavens.

Looking back across the common,
to earth unploughed for millennia
where thousands and thousands
of bird tracks scored the mud,

and glistered in the sun
that was dropping over Wolvercote.

Catalunya

Christ of Taüll

Go, he said, *and for an hour just stand and look.*
I stared into the face, recalling the story

of a murder one morning after mass:
the rain-worn steps of a limestone cathedral,

a scene tended by my mother, her words
embossed a bitterness in breath.

As a girl she was told how they tried
to staunch the wound, the lead slug

fingered at but irretrievable, tiny
bubbles bursting at the corner of his mouth.

Ego sum lux mundi, by the Christ of Taüll
I saw the face at first then no face at all.

Carrer Sant Pau

Whatever was left of that other life
I laid it out on the Carrer Sant Pau:

a ticket stub, a matchbook, a key fob,
piece by piece I offered it all up.

Naked on the tiles she traced a black
line around her eye, pink circles

on her knees when she stood, her skin
a warm citrine, I lay watching on the sheets.

Later, her quick tongue, hot and drunk.
I called her by another's name, we fought,

made love again, urgent for each other,
as if my hands might pass right through her.

The Evening Sea

Blanes, the train delayed,
heat-sheen on the plastic bucket seats

the glad hour almost upon us
when the colours of the waves

are tender and vast.
I looked to the sea and thought

of the forest fire last summer:
pine trunks scorched black

car alarms, petrol tanks blowing out,
how we ran down to the shore,

smoke rolling in like fog,
erasing every one of us.

A Herring Famine

The Drift

Buoys from bladders
of pigs and bullocks
mark the fleet nets:

a curtain hung
below the water
at sundown bright

shapes feeding
at the surface,
the herring boat swung in

the prevailing wind,
and left to drift
through the night,

stars on the water
like the silver darlings
who fed there earlier.

A Supper Song

Thinner and scarcer,
thinner and scarcer,
the table set for supper

hard bread, a smur of butter.
The new nets do not mend it
she sends them back up empty.

The table set for supper
hard bread, a smur of butter.

Trafford Park

How far then to this:
I want to draw a line,
on this borrowed

municipal map,
to trace the skaffie
of family legend

making its way south.
The sea empty of fish,
I want to watch them

finally arrived,
at the new house –
the 'Village' with its

freshly consecrated
churches, clinics,
clubhouse, washhouse,

newness like a curse,
its taint on everything.
Streets of cable makers,

masons, machinists;
to ask the pale faces
who stand arrayed

in this fading photograph
clear-eyed and tense
what it was to be so

definitively delivered from
a wild and known coast,
to clean lines of the future:

aerodrome, a production
line for hundreds of thousands
of Model Ts.

At night under
electric light, over
indoor plumbing

if they felt the skill
slowly bleeding
from their fingers,

how to thread
a net or weave
a creel, gauge with

wooden measures
or scatter rough salt
as other motions

were learned,
on the vastnesses
of factory floors.

If those instincts
bred in them so long
became suddenly

redundant.

Did the sea
linger in their dreams
so far inland,

gulls gathered
west of the harbour
the feeding flocks

dunes and fossil cliffs,
the bittern, the little owl
the bee eater,

the gorse mounds
and the houses
looking east.

How many nights
here in their
new home did

they dream of
herring in their
glittering millions?

Pawnbrokers

DELUGE OF PANIC
SELLING OVERWHELMS
THE MARKET

and currents
ran fast beyond
their making.

My great uncle,
a clever,
breathless boy,

plagued by sores,
who never wept
when bathed

in salt water – simply
repeated *nicey nicey*
over and over –

runs down the alley
behind the street his
mother walks along

humming three bars
of an old song
from a fireside, from *before.*

He's learned to keep up –
to time his arrival
to accord with hers –

prince of the ginnels
and newly laid lanes
he struggles under

the weight,
the sweat, the smoke,
of all the family's winter coats.

Remains

What lasts?

After the slums were
declared then cleared
and the factories shut,

weed-strewn wrecks
bolted, chain-linked
bomb-scarred, emptied,

the future
lapsed beyond recognition
into the simple past.

I stand where they arrived
and take stock.
Haul up these nets

and find clam-shells,
oil cans, old iron,
stories about being

poor and the shame
that no wealth
would ever erase.

I pitch my ear
into the pulsing air
that hangs

around the empty
space, and hear those
last songs

that lodged
with us, their lost
and rightful inheritors.

Sulphur

Long before midday the fierce heat that summer
had us pinned in the corners of the converted
grain store, sweating it out, man and wife,
eyeing each other like traitors,

all through that long stretch in stasis
as light moved up the whitewashed wall
we waited for the day to cool, the bands to start up:
Europop welcome home the diaspora.

The birds worked themselves into our dreams
screaming chicks scratching in the rafters,
the frantic, scrabbling footfall on the boards
the absolute pitch of their terror, a wanting

we might have recognised as our own. In those
months the commonplace became miraculous;
the blown rose of Palermo or driving late
on narrow roads past abandoned sulphur mines.

Climbing the *calvario* each evening at dusk,
so far inland the distant communes felt like islands,
the hawks that bred there baring their wings,
like our boredom, taking to the air.

We would wake in the night to noises from the fields
beyond the Purgatory Church where it was said
they injected stallions with cocaine and raced them,
frothing, teeth bared, wild-eyed in the darkness.

The Caracalla Baths

Mussolini staged operas in these tunnels.
Perhaps there is a cult we each construct, a room

where every carelessness, unkindness, cruelty,
each bitter kiss, each fumbled, flickering lust

lives. Ignoring the tour group,
you turn into the chamber with its wide flanks,

its space for stretching out at a banquet,
glance at the pit in which a drugged bull –

the low mewling, the slipping hooves –
was led to a metal grill, muscled throat slashed.

Below the grill a niche. You recognise the need
to crawl on hands and knees, initiate, deep into it,

to be drenched with hot, unstopping blood.

Ghost Ranch

'Because there were no flowers I began picking up bones'
– GEORGIA O'KEEFFE

Glance from the barrel where the bones are bled,
to the other landscapes before this one made sense:

white-aproned girl walking through Sun Prairie, Wisconsin.
With Stieglitz, in the snow, as Manhattan

towered around you, and the wind thrashed his cape.
In repose at a high window, shouldering a form,

the city light working its way around your face.
Now your days are spent here by the Plaza Blanca cliffs

the badlands near Abiquiú, the white place;
the abandoned hacienda, your private mountain.

God said if you painted it you could possess it.
Before your sight finally goes, I see you walking out

among the bones – that silent care, collecting for
Ram's Head White Hollyhock and Little Hills.

Inner Harbor

for A.M.

Proper to have crossed the Susquehanna
to find you teaching elegy in a city of two hundred

recent murders: bludgeoned outside Crazy Ray's
or shot in the back running from Wolfe Liquors.

Your library seemed a kind of answer, a dukedom large enough
a black-flanked wood-burner and life of Wordsworth.

We ate blue crab and fried oysters in an empty restaurant
where they knew you, rain-light on the cranes outside,

recalling for my wife the last words of your father.
You were younger here somehow, a man returned.

I thought of John Wollaston, his satchel of raw pigment
in pigs' bladders and glass syringes, old brushes,

arrived now at these shores, with a new name to make,
and riding out along the eastern sea-board.

A Mother

By her master's workshop near the motorway
stiff-hipped, swollen with another litter,

she walks twice in a circle then settles
in the shadow of a rusted pick-up,

where she watches your mother's shack:
as you emerge from the ply-board interior,

its fly-blown cooker, filthy blankets,
push-chair filled with rolled-up rush mats,

a shoe-box of cassettes, a guitar, unstringed,
hanging on the wall from when your mother

was once capable of love and being present.
Your hair thick with lice, blinking in the sunlight

you wander, purposeless, thin-limbed
belly distended among the failed cars,

and petrol slicks, the desert air
hunger growing tightly coiled inside you.

I do not know how this begins,
what brings her shuffling over, head down

heavy with her unborn, blind litter, nosing
around your hand, lying on her side.

How she offers or you know to take, her teat
is not miraculous, you did not have to know or ask.

From the Deep End

Tomorrow this will all be boarded up: soon
the drained pool clumped with willow herb,

a slick rat scuttling back along tiles
Sunny Lowry swam above in girlhood:

she stands barefoot on the beach in darkness
on the other side England lies, sleeping.

Mizzle over white cliffs, she emerges from the bay
whipped raw by jellyfish, burning but

strong as a drayman, arms of cartwright,
aviatrix goggles and her neat white cap

that saved her life when the support boat lost
her, in lightning, the last attempt abandoned

by the fading glow of Folkstone –
her bare knees and the shouts of *Harlot*.

Place it all in here before it closes,
once washhouse, once bath house, once crucible

of dreams for a strong girl
swimming through the night across the channel.

Six Scenes from a Marriage

Tir an Eòrna

My love is alone on the summer island of her childhood:
a girl leaning against a bicycle on a treeless hill at dusk.
I want to speak to her then, not now. Between Hynish
and Sandaig and all the places I have never been, pausing
to watch the waves, the white wall of the CalMac shrinking
in the distance. I want to write my way back into this love.
To meet her newly resident in silence, in long hours of light,
alone with the prayers and sandwich pastes of her aged aunt;
to come to her softly as rain or wind moving through the barley.

Machir Bay

Fierce wind on the white sands and the oyster-blue last light
a house crouched on the headland, and you striding out
hands deep in your pockets. I loved you then, by all
the power and simple rage of the moiling lead-lined sea,
boggy hollow and the rushing sands, and your wish to be
alone, however vast already was your aloneness, through
spinning drifts and snaking waves, the bitter cold at our faces,
raw when we returned to the car and the courtesy light
clicked on, and we saw ourselves, what we'd become.

Friedrichshain-Kreuzberg

Anxious in the line for Berghain that winter I was worried
I would somehow betray you; a look, a misplaced gesture:
I followed you through gritted streets, old snow, to that long
mirthless queue, the vast blank building, thick with anticipation,
I watched as three Americans in Armani were turned away.
In the turbine hall I thought of Dante's circles of hell,
of the room a floor below where lust was explicated endlessly.
We moved together in the cavernous dark, the smoke,
a catastrophe of bodies, beneath the rituals of disappearance.

Glenlyon

I am writing to your absence, to those casual vast gulfs
to the distances which open up between us; those rifts
to the places in which I am unable to reach you or
when I confound myself and burn with anger –
I am remembering that walk in the rain and early dark
thirty yards or so to the kirk. The tinsel freshly hung
for the Christmas service and us quickly married. A tree
had fallen at the mouth of the glen. They sawed it open,
waved us through. Define us by our distances again.

Campo Bandiera e Moro

Black-mouthed, black-tongued, black-lipped, squid ink;
a litre of rough white wine pumped into a plastic bottle
like piss or contraband petrol. Woozy on the vaporetto
the windows thick with condensation en route to the airport.
Your taste on my tongue, a sweet stain wreathing my hands;
it's raining again, but I cannot capture you through all
the vanishing acts of a marriage: so I trace you back to
the room before we left, sound of church bells, looking out
to a boy in a blue cagoule chasing a bird across the square.

Envoi

I offer these as charms, as scars,
     as maps back to a love
as perhaps it never was, to all its
     fractured, broken modes.
     Who thought that it would come to this
that day to day, we could persist.

A History Lesson

This is where it culminates, here
in concertinas of yellowed paper:
a rotten accordion of laundry bills,
sump of chits, syllabuses, inventories
boxed and forgotten, a shifting desert

of manila, history collapsing on itself,
massing in the storeroom under the stage.

But the sound of the children, who
congregate each morning, still
reaches here where all is said and done.
The tracks and traces of the girls just up,
all vanished now, thin memories, at best.

But who, like those above, wanted then
so fiercely for life to come to them.

Dorothea Beale's Death Mask

The same face that frowns out from the photograph
beside Empress Frederick, like two plump rooks at roost
each a singular stern mass of black gloss in their pomp –

(early that May morning, in the college she had founded, I stood
on the lawn promising I would tell him. As quietly,
to herself almost, she said she wasn't sure it was his, she'd lost it,
whatever it was or might have been

I remember how the sound of the choir from the tower
came down, then birdsong, and rain faint on leaves above us)

how it reprimands me now.

The Beekeeper

No one saw Josef Guzy, in smock and veil,
collapse beside the painted barn: only smoke
rising from the toppled fire-pot.

Wisniewski told how when the doctor arrived
from a lunch of kielbasa, boiled eggs, butter,
a second glass of Żubrówka with bison herb,

he found the pale body pulseless, cooling,
wife and daughter sobbing. Offered
condolences and brief prayer. Later as the

funeral director unsealed the silk-lined casket
to retrieve a chain, of sentimental value,
his knuckles brushed an artery and it throbbed,

the next week he found on his doorstep
the stopped heart of a single jar of honey.

The Weatherman

after Evgenia Arbugaeva

As you gather firewood by the empty lighthouse
a torch beam cuts the air above the tundra,

you kick snow from your boots as you re-enter
the wooden cabin, home out on the peninsula.

On your desk a photograph of Yuri Gagarin,
data tables, two biscuits, a light bulb,

a bronze ashtray, a crumpled cigarette butt.
By night you build watch-towers out of matchsticks

as if to better survey the expanse of your solitude:
a man stood a whole day at a window watching rain

as if it were the question that answered all others.
How easily you shed your self, become the Arctic wind,

the snowstorm that will delay tonight's transmission.
A thousand miles south, Moscow awaits your data.

Raketa

Made in Russia, a factory with its own
Department of Propaganda.

Your first gift, my love, your last.
You strapped it to my wrist.

I wind it up each night,
and in your absence, hear it tick.

A Quaker Burial Ground

Leave the salt marsh swards
    grazed and submerged
on the high spring tides.

Scurvy grass, sea aster, thrift.

The sea lavender inland
    dying north of Ravenglass.
Abandon the white beaked sedge of the raised bogs.

Cranberry, sundew,
the verges of dwarf gorse, wild chamomile
the limestone crossings, rock rose.

Spring cinquefoil,
    spotted cat's ear,
       fragrant orchid.

Letting go,
    forget each name:
                a blank
until you reach the burial ground.

Death should always look like this –

a plain field and a high stone wall.
    Three words unmake the world:
earth and stone and sky.

Night Flight

Deserts, wild woods, glaciers
three thousand miles of ocean
two of us, complete strangers,
sleeping, shoulder to shoulder.

The Leap

We walked to the gorge through dense heat,
ancient shade, pine, mimosa, dragonflies,
babies strapped like flour sacks to our fronts.

Your husband first from the Roman bridge
the arch high as a double decker bus,
then you, a lit match, one arm outstretched.

Your daughter at the river's edge, her hot cheeks,
her mother plunging then gone
in the cold pool, the endless dark.

And when you surfaced, her tears stopped
and we who watched knew all there was of loss,
of stepping off, of how a life

is lived in the reflection of our falling
in the eyes of those we love.

Spam

And just when you had unlearned
each cadence of her name,
her face no more troubled you
in bars or crowded shopping streets,
no more questions woke you
on the edge of sleep:
                              there she is
her abandoned address, glowing
home to some cipher selling
valium, viagra, xanex, sex.
A sloughed husk, an empty shell,
hold it to your ear and hear the ocean.

Xeno-Canto

Vanished from the grasslands and
the edges the empty iceless Arctic

when no trace remains but jpegs,
glitchy footage on a flash drive,

a server in a room somewhere,
kept on at the whim of its inheritor

a whirring fan, technology lapsing
byte by byte into deeper obsolescence.

Picture them, before the world emptied
in Uttarakhand, Aquitaine, Roccabruna

recording those species that remained:
Sunset, Miramar, Bernabe Lopez-Lanus

raising his phone like a thurible
At the backs of 'Costanera' buildings.

Two birds preparing to rest.

The Devil's Festival

Not the dazzle of cut glass or the diamonds
or the waiters flown in from Switzerland,
boys who had never left their home valley
(eating sausage and stale bread on the train to the airport)
the golf links and fairway, the club for royalty,
the quails' eggs stuffed with golden caviar,
the roast peacocks, champagne sorbet,
the presence of Emperor Haile Selassie,
the great five-pronged star of the tent city
and the military aeroplanes loaded with ice
but the thousands of sparrows, imported,
the pipe-cleaner feet, blunt seeds of their beaks
in miles of freshly planted pines and cedar trees
dropping softly as ash flakes or a first snow.

Apples

'I do not think he's a bad man but he's left us without a son.'

I do not know which myth this fits –
I cannot name an oil painting hanging
in a gallery where two boys lie dead
unmarked across a mass of perfect fruit.

There is something of the fall, of course, but
I recognise in the news report a fissure
as the epic collapses to an ordinary sadness:
the apples were for the Marden Fruit Show –

The financial prizes were very modest . . .
It was the kudos of winning that was more important.

Stoop

'The hardest thing of all to see is what is really there'
– J. A. BAKER

Gripped now
by its bottle-glass throat
from the slick
mess of viscera and bone

you untangle sealed
and living parts
like wires from
the back of a shattered radio.

And to what costs
might we go to hold
that savage part so close –
a man arrested at Heathrow

eggs bandaged to his breast, like bombs,
on a plane bound for Dubai.

Hôtel Idéal Séjour

The winter sea and perhaps
in the distance the sound of waves.

The women at your bedside
are dressed against the chill.

And you, trussed for a hernia,
weeks of watching each centime,

that dinner where they gathered
to send you back a second time.

Laughter, some soft words,
the clearing of a throat;

George adjusts her watch,
Edith flattens down her skirts.

What warrens, what romances
resonate and echo through

your dreaming mind, what irks
the dying child inside?

Your breathing thins, then stops.
They watch you through the night to come.

Swifts at Saint-Cézaire

Thunder over the valley then
swifts sudden on the heavy air

we watched from the borrowed home
together now after years alone

as if that archive of our past lives burned –
fragments of parchment ash they rose.

At Sea

I.

This is my first commission out of Dartmouth;
    our grey ship ploughs the water of the North Atlantic.
The captain locked like frozen cargo below deck.
    After weeks of silence about his erratic behaviour,
came his hysterical screaming one evening at supper,
    in the gloom of the wardroom the ship's doctor
and I whispered like schoolboys up past our curfew.
    In temporary command I issued an order to ram
the shadow we spotted that morning to starboard.
    We watched the crew fishing corpses of submariners,
interring their faces inside me. Shaped to defend an Empire,
    they will reward me with a piece of paper:
a telegram from the King will sit on my desk,
    saluting me, regretting he couldn't be there in person.

II.

Hostilities over they sent me to the Führer's yacht:
  her broad deck polished like the floor of a ballroom.
We motored out into the Mediterranean,
  the gaunt crew sunbathing like honeymooners,
reacquainting themselves, slowly, with pleasure.
  That night in a commissioned act of forgetting,
we tossed his enigma machines overboard,
  like unwanted bycatch, into the ocean.
Rotors that carried orders to each theatre of war:
  fire bombed cathedral cities, filled cattle trucks
with shivering children, wiped villages off maps,
  barnacle now like bones or sunken treasure.
She was towed to a torpedo station in Narragansett
  and stripped, her frail hull breached over and over.

Ice

A girl is eating an ice lolly in
Old Lyme, Connecticut in 1937
on a wide porch with cedar shingles.
Beyond her is tall grass, some
thistles, three cows, the ocean

which she walks to each morning
and looks north-east to Scotland
or a touch above due east to Europe
where a future is fermenting
that will come for her brother

who sits on the staircase beside her
in boyhood, though not for much longer,
unaware of this, eating his ice lolly,
in the sunshine, that summer.

A Manse in Fife

The accretions of a lifetime,
a black and white battleship at anchor
fading in a frame above the barometer,
in the room where they would breakfast.

Shelling peas into a plastic tub
a dry lawn, the lavender loud with bees,
his beer brewing in its bucket
a walnut tree in fruit, his reddened hand
brings down its lowest branch.

Empty now, the carpets taken up
the window frames painted every summer
flaking, the clock in his office stopped,
on the Life Boat calendar, his last day struck off.

The Sleeper Train

I.

Midnight at
the equinox

a lounge car's
faded saltires,

musk of bodies
eau de cologne,

Embassy cigarettes,
the Midlands'

haze of orange
lights on black

drinking with a
surgeon, tongues

loosening to grief
through potted

histories of field
hospitals, clinics

canvas tents,
malarial places

his young hands
one around a

stranger's heart
pumped too hard.

Grotesque, he said,
the blood. So much,

the mops slapping
as they cleared it up.

II.

Foetal on the
top bunk of

a lilac berth
you dreamt

that night of
another train

moving east
through Africa;

of teak dhows,
salt-hardened

sails, bodies
of boys falling,

an okra sea
a skinny turkey

from Manda.
New Year; tango

an Italian-owned
hotel, fireworks

the beachfront
home

where a crippled
woman slept

from pangas
they would come

with machine pistols
after you left.

A Caddis Fly

tied with elk hair
and hare's fur –

the trout came
glistening up

the clockwork
of its mouth

a miracle –
your brother

brought the big
rock down,

this living thing
cracked and

spasmed
in your hand.

The Tower

A train on the viaduct
runs its rope of light
    out towards the Pennines

the missing, the buried
dead of Saddleworth
    the silent, trespassed acres.

A rising wind, then a keening
sound from the
    tower's glass fins.

Starved of sleep
in their condos. You tell me
    the story of your father

his life's diminuendo.
The tower sings,
    ministering to the dead,

in abandoned rooms
crying from the cholera
    pits by the Medlock.

Children of Little Ireland
faces of famished mothers
    bright among the fern stems.

Hellebore

What would I have said to disrupt
the life I coveted? There was nothing,
so there is nothing now to miss.
You are a year away, receding into myth:

I make you now the gift of this; a hellebore
Christmas Rose, drug of Dionysus,
false man, untier, goat killer, lord.
The daughters of the King of Argos

stream naked through the city, weeping.

Two Wedding Poems

Inked

for Apphia and George

on the tender vellum
of his hand –

three letters –
your given names,

uneven as text
on a Roman coin,

a storekeeper
in Santa Monica

mistook them for
a gang sign.

To remove it now
would leave a scar

roughly the size
of a human heart.

Stunts

for Heather and Neal

Her father
holds her by the wrist

out over the dam, as
the Nicaraguan sisters

from her neighbourhood,
shriek, blindfolded by

their own small hands.
Before he pulls her back,

let's pause that afternoon,
sun high, rattle snakes

coiled in the long grass
a million gallons

of white water
silent now in California.

The Good Neighbour

We did not know your name but watched
all year from that tower block in Ardwick
your belt tightening notch by notch, like a garotte.
Your wasted pallor, scarecrow demeanour,
that matted mass of unwashed hair
hanging like a snared pelt to your coccyx.

Begging *al fresco* if the good weather lingered.
We watched your body thinning, your face's
sharpening planes, skin's shades of builder's sand,
then the plain yellow of a sick man, your stink
unwashed, old sweat, fox shit, dead dog.
We wondered aloud what your story was –

noted a certain rectitude in the shambling walk –
a hint of the busy-body, imagined a mother
prominent in a village, a sitter on committees.
We thought you atavistic, a throwback,
as you became your own wax-work.
Your flat, four floors above, nested with needles,

newspaper at the windows, a reptile incubating.
You were never anything but polite to us
though once we even wished you dead
not moving slowly across the car park at dusk
not telling us about the night just spent at a rave,
bouncing on a mattress, giggling, famine-stricken.

Once I refused to get into the lift with you –
pretending there might not be enough room –
I watched you grow angry then desperate –
the sick man, the good neighbour shouting,
then pleading, and pleading, as if we continued
believing this were all normal, it could be.

The Dark Star

*'Preparations were in hand for the installation of integral
sanitation in one wing'* – THE WOOLF REPORT,
STRANGEWAYS PRISON, 1991

I. BEFORE THE RIOT

The dark star, sleeping.
Shadows hang in the wings
of the human warehouse,
a hive of sixteen hundred
souls, three to a cell,
boys scratching under blankets
dreaming of Eccles & Hyde
cycling the East Lancs Road
the reservoir at Dovestone,
a mother's mottled arms,
red-tipped fishing lures,
the canal, of carp, roach,
bumper cars, a carousel,
candyfloss, a long deep kiss,
a mouth parted, in the half-light
cherubic, in the corner
of the cell a lidless
plastic bucket of piss

II. START OF THE RIOT

Chapel
the army preacher
gospel of St Paul

Sinners words
pass through the crowd
not when or now or how,
just this, that   change in pressure before a thunderstorm

with sticks and hoods on the
vestry stairs – they wait silent as altar boys at prayer.

Chaplain rises to announce the final hymn
as a single prisoner runs down the aisle.

Balaclavas, chair legs from their trousers . . .
this sequestered, skin-warmed wood will wound.

Light explodes behind the preacher's eyes.

III. SIEGE

C-Wing.
Home of the special prisoners,
they tear their doors off the hinges
drag them to the walk-in freezer –
as if their flesh might perish
as if to better preserve them for what's coming.
Iron bars. Frenzy.
Soft flesh breaking against bone,
skulls split like antique oak,
the eggshell of a shattered eye socket
they pull the last arrival from his cell by his hair,
beat him with sticks like a mule
lift him in the air like a groom at his wedding
throw him over the railings.

And when he clings,
stamp his fingertips
to bruised berries.
And when he falls
lob tables and chairs down to bury him.

*

All cells opened by a single set of keys.

Paul clenched the stem of red rose in his teeth
foster homes from seven and a half,
then checkbook fraud, now this . . .

Alan Lord
scaling the rotunda scaffolding
breaks through boards and beams
tearing and punching his way
up to slates
to weak sun, pigeons,
a grey muscle of rain
flexing on the Pennines
acres of untainted air,
the Arndale and the CIS
glow softly in the distance.

*

Trapeze artists, wing-walkers,
Acrobats each man discovering a head for heights.

Festival. Circus. Theatre. Performance piece.
Rain-swept rooftop carnival. Macabre. Unsafe.

This whole place is unsafe.

*

It's raining slates again
from a slate sky
an intermittent arrow shower each afternoon.
Most miss, some hit . . .
in the place
the threats come from
the shouts of
just wait until we get you down.
A guard collapses under his shield
clutching his chin, it hangs
on a split string of sinew and shattered bone.

Then down
            come
the

coping stones

IV. MEDIA REPORTING

Paul –
his throat raw through a sawn-off traffic cone
as the sirens drown him out

Alan Lord says look at
the blackboard and only the blackboard.
The cameraman pans then zooms from the building opposite
a helicopter tilts, circles, lifts

Extracts from
The Stoppage of Letters Book
chalked word by word
guards in the bar each lunch hour
returning to the wings – pints of Heavy in them –
    punishments, beatings on a whim –
Alan Lord chalks up the
words of sons whose mothers never heard them.

Until the water cannons aim at him.

V. CONCLUSIONS

It is so late now it is early –
Alan captured.

(As somewhere in the English countryside an illegal rave
    winds down -
the parked up banks of Astras and Cortinas depart:
    this is the silence of that empty field,
    pocked with cans and reverb from a blown PA)

Rage has thinned to pity.

Five left.
Marooned above the carcass
of the building as it smolders.

In the distance Manchester
goes about its business
    blue smoke from chimneys,
    contrails from an airbus out of Ringway
    a hundred office blocks light up.

Lifted down in the bucket
of the cherry picker –
you might think for a moment they were saved.

The motion heroic, an arc recognisable from fantasies of rescue –
the visual grammar
of stranded cats or babies lifted safe from burning buildings.

Notice how their fists are raised.
For a moment they might be
exiting some elevated place   a stadium   a final encore
to the roar of thousands of massed fans.

Look now at their faces, their victory as it vanishes.
The terror of what awaits them.
Their giving up – in the end – for their mothers
who called up to the youngest from behind the broadcast vans
John-John.
Oh John Come Down Now Lad It's Daylight. And everybody's here.

An Essay on Perspective

A girl with a broken nose and a styrofoam cup
sits crossed-legged by the underpass

and watches as behind the palace walls
a breeze moves through the sycamores.

Snapshots

Here is the poem I could never get right.
The one where your face is pixilated,
bearded, weary,
        native until your
voice betrays you.

Where we talk about the photographs you sent:

two snarling mastiffs,
the dead-weight
of their massive heads,
ears and tails razored to nubs,
        the arena in winter,
            blue shadows of the Hindu Kush.

Or the confectioner
        his factory's furnace-heat
and squalor
that viscous mixture
        slung up on hooks.

Like what? Like guts. The poem where I want to guess and
    tell you how,

At night you hear the dead file past your door.
The boy with his face half burned away:
                lips shorn, those tiny shattered pegs of teeth,
who lisps your name, then asks you where you've been.

But when I read these lines to you, home now, on your sofa
in the summer, you're safe again, and the words are gone.

Henbane

First the dark aches
pains in the belly and
blistering bowels,

fingernails flake away
like almonds, blanched
moon-white, everything

tender to the touch.
Night wild inside you,
new hurt, shattered

spars of bone, as shrews
and moorhens quiver in
their nests, the earth sinks

under your feet,
the hutch-stink of the soul,
an anchor chain,

in a port an hour away
rushing over a gunnel,
snarling as it falls,

a sea without a shore.

At Café Loup

I run a finger
        over my left breast,
to trace again
        a ragged line –
of sutures,
        blackened
butterfly stitch,
        that seals
        a brand new
emptiness.

Red wine stains
        your teeth and lips
but on your tongue,
        if asked, I'd guess
                that what you taste
is human flesh.

The Boundary Line

i.m. H.L.

A rainless English summer afternoon –
at one end of our primary school's

parched wicket, your batting partner;
I watch you hit a ball so clean and high

it sails across the boundary line.
We must, I guess, be ten years old or less

and have known each other all our lives.
I follow its flight and it leads me on

to those men you might have become:
an actor with young Elvis looks,

a cricketer of the more refined sort
or if your wilder side had reigned:

an art thief lifting gilt-frames
over laser beams, a litigate, a lawyer

a lay preacher, these vestiges,
the lives unlived, hung like costumes

your many warehoused selves,
mothballed, on hold.

*

I lost sight of you for a decade or so
but home sometimes would catch you

walking in to work, carelessly shaven
a little heavier but recognisable:

that tight-eyed smirk
the wildfire of your laughter

first person I ever saw jet-lagged
dozing in front of the Grand National

in a warm room at my grandma's house
a walk along the river to the woods

in which we fashioned weapons,
old tins and cans and iron poles, stink of vetch

wild garlic, water-logged rugby pitches,
dog shit, mud, smeared allotment glass,

Medieval things we dared not touch.
Take all of this. Take all of you

back through that half-life before
visiting you in hospital the first time

your gentleness untainted, that sly kindness,
that recourse always to humour,

those weeks when we had just left school,
you mimed breaking an egg over a sunbathing girl,

that seam of the untameable, the ordered world
all affect, in need of tearing through

the time you rabbit-punched an older boy
we were chased across a Cumbrian town

hiding in a woman's house as they came
with screaming brothers, scenting blood.

In foreign cities I often picture you;
a bar in Montmartre, signalling another glass,

joining in a song or a game of dominoes
waiting on a girl to finish her shift,

who will ride pillion to an attic room
in the eighteenth arrondissement,

where your next novel or some
ambitious symphony lies unwritten

by a forest of empty wine bottles
and letters home you never posted.

Every year friends walk to your tree;
you would have liked the rabble but

laughed too, whispered some cutting
remark, taken it too far, had us all in tears.

The last time I saw you we shared
a cigarette, spot-lit by white plastic

chairs in a rain-drenched suburban garden
you had just won hundreds on a horse

I saw the good luck spooked you -
not long after I heard the news

that you had gone: to think of you falling
is to think always of the ball you struck

sailing higher, out beyond the school
through those banks of August cloud

red leather and cork a meteor spun out
in reverse and sailing plain across

the universe into a silence that is unending
through that dense nothing which awaits us all.

Notes

'A Herring Famine': Trafford Park was the world's first planned industrial estate. My mother's family, fishermen from Aberdeen, came to Manchester to take up work there during one of the 'herring famines' from which this collection takes its title.

'The Weatherman': a series of photographs by Evgenia Arbugaeva of Vyacheslav Korotki, a Russian meteorologist living on the Barents Sea.

'Inner Harbor': John Wollaston was an English painter of portraits, active in the British colonies in North America.

'From the Deep End': Levenshulme Baths closed in 2016.

'Catalunya': the Absis de Sant Climent de Taüll is a Romanesque fresco in the Museu Nacional d'Art de Catalunya painted in the early twelfth century.

'The Dark Star': a local name for Strangeways prison, designed by architect Alfred Waterhouse, famous for its panopticon design.

'The Devil's Festival': the name given by Ayatollah Khomeini to the lavish celebration held in 1971 by Shah Reza Pahlavi to mark the twenty-five-hundred-year anniversary of the Persian Empire.

'Apples': in 2013 two Hampshire farm workers died retrieving apples for a fruit show from a nitrogen-filled store. Instead of using a net or a hooked pole, they entered through a small hatch in the roof. The process – known as 'scuba diving' – involved holding their breath while they retrieved the apples.

'Xeno-Canto': a database of bird sounds from the around the world.

'Hôtel Idéal Séjour': the boarding house on the French Riviera where W.B. Yeats spent his final days.

'At Sea': two memories from my paternal grandfather.

Acknowledgements

Thanks to Parisa Ebrahimi and Clara Farmer at Chatto & Windus for their work on this book. Thanks also to Edmund Gordon for his encouragement and close reading.